MAKE A POWERFUL POINT

To Make a POWERFUL Point, we have to understand what works. We need to practice some art and science to use PowerPoint to persuade.

I've broken this down into "10 Simple Rules to Avoid Bad PowerPoint Karma and Have a Leadership Conversation." I can tell you it took me a long time to settle on that title. I got a lot of pushback from colleagues and friends. The words rules, karma, and leadership conversation were all troublesome.

Rules work. I thought of words like "commandment," "mandate" and "structure" – but I "ruled" them all out. Too strong. Too dictatorial. You can't mindlessly follow these ten simple rules. Sure they're good guidelines, but there are too many variables out there for all ten to work all the time. I don't want you to become the victim of unintended consequence. Likewise, "guide," "tip" and "hint" didn't make the cut. Much too soft.

These rules are here because they work. Use them to help you. Think about how they apply to the context you're in. By all means ignore them if you want to – but have a good reason in mind for doing so.

Karma was difficult. I do believe people inherit their PowerPoint karma. We get out of presenting what we put into it – and for a lot of people, that isn't much. We all see this – boring PowerPoint, setting a standard of tedious slides full of bullets and the odd piece of clip-art. And we all play, reusing old slides, borrowing from other bad presentations.

The leadership conversation is the reason that you are up there presenting. A presentation is the one planned leadership moment you have. It's a precious opportunity to persuade and make a positive impact on your audience. It is a leadership moment; one that you should not squander.

10 RULES

Rule #1
Know What You Want to Achieve

The surest sign your presentation is off to a bad start: you open up PowerPoint and start typing. Rookie mistake. Here's why — if you don't make it relevant to them, audiences don't care — no matter how you dress it up.

A good presentation is a dialogue, not a monologue. It's a journey. A conversation between people. For that to happen, you have to interest the audience and get them involved. That's not going to happen if you make the presentation about you (a monologue), instead of about them (a dialogue).

So, Baron von Ruthless,* if you have monologuing tendencies, Rule #1 is for you.

A good presentation starts with two simple questions:

> *What do I want to get across?*

> *What do they (the audience) want?*

If you can answer those you have a ***chance*** of pulling off a good presentation.

ı

---

*Baron von Ruthless, the supervillain in the movie The Incredibles. He predictably lost his advantage over our hero, as he launched into his monologue about ruling the world. Also see all James Bond villains ever.

Get a plan approved

What do I want?

1. Show progress against the 2011 PLAN

2. Engineering Group understands and is tracking towards the future we need to create

Report status

3. I am not just an engineer, I see the fit in a business context and could be a potential CEO here

Sell an idea

What does BOB want?   HEATHER MARTINE

1. See Where missed revenue commitments come from

↖ that we aren't repeating the same mistakes

2. Understand Relevance of new product releases to market

3. Get "under the hood" to understand the new product

Ask your audience what they want.
OR ask someone else.
OR guess!
But when you begin, ask them anyway

Figuring out what you want to achieve and then using it as a guide and a filter is simple. First, get a scrap piece of paper. A napkin will do. Draw a line down the middle, dividing the paper into two columns. On the left, write down the outcomes I want. On the right, write down what the audience needs?

Think hard. Ruthlessly prioritize. You've just won a promotion. You have the first Ops review. Your Region President and the CEO will be there. What do you want? If you're honest, not making any career ending mistakes might be on your wish list. But maybe not at the top. You want to show up well. Have them believe they made a good choice in promoting you. Let them know the plan for your piece of the business. Whatever it is, be honest with yourself. Rank. Focus on what's important to you.

Now move to the right hand column. Here you will put down what the audience needs. The best way to get that information is to ask the audience directly, in advance. If it's your first Ops review, ask your boss for some advice. "What do you want to come out of this knowing?" "Are there any particular aspects you want me to cover in depth?" You will usually get a candid answer. After all, that person has a vested interest in you succeeding.

If you can't get to them, ask someone else. A peer or a colleague. Find a good stand-in. If you have no other options, (and this is a place of last resort) guess. Thinking about it will do you some good. In your Ops review, they will probably want to know that you have a solid handle on the business. They want to understand how you are doing against plan; and in any areas that fall short, how you are going to make up the gap.

We've designed a template to help you. It goes further than the two column list, and challenges you. How do you want the audience to feel after your presentation, what do you want them to know and what do you want them to do? On the right, it's about how they feel coming into the presentation, what they want to know and what the audience is prepared to do.

T-Leaf

What do I want them to...   What do they want to...

Who are THEY? Write their name.

Feel?
1.
2.
3.

Know?
1.
2.
3.

Do?
1.
2.
3.

That's it. You're done with rule one. You know what you want to achieve. Don't throw that scrap piece of paper away. This is your north star. As you dive into the work of pulling your presentation together, check against it. It will help you create and prune your work.

Rule #2
It's All About Me

Think about it. Social media exploits this egocentric view of the world. How many friends do you have? Likes? Followers? Brands tap into it too. Intel has the Museum of Me. Nike logs how many miles you run (or don't in my case). Coke has stirred a narcissistic frenzy by unveiling a can with your name on it. A central tenet of gamification is how many badges you've collected and how you're scoring against your peers.

"Me" is our favorite conversation.

If you don't remember that, you might as well be speaking to an empty room. There are two sides to every conversation. It's your job to make sure that the person or persons you are talking to are willing and able to hear what you have to say. Just because you have 30 minutes on an agenda to ramble on about your favorite subject doesn't mean anyone has to listen. It only means they have to sit there and pretend to. That's why in Rule #1 you made your guide and dedicated 50% of the available space to what other people wanted to hear. Refer to this. What does the audience want? Give it to them.

So if you are out there selling what your company can do for someone, remember this: They're not interested in your company, or its storied credentials. What they want is the solution to their business problem. Can you help with that? Do you understand what they are going through? The challenges they face?

Can you make their job easier? Can you make them the hero that saves millions to the bottom line or wrestles with the dragon of workforce communication? Rolling out a new initiative or project? Who does it affect? Why will it make their jobs easier? Their lives better? What's in it for them?

You have to make it about them. This isn't just psychobabble. We can mathematically prove this. If we plot how interested a member of the audience is, against how much it is about them, using the formula where interest = $all(me)^2 + I$, we see a curve where interest exponentially increases, the more it's about me.

Clearly, down at the bottom of the curve, when it isn't about me, I am not very interested. Up at the top, when it's all about me, I am very interested. We call this phenomenon the slope of increasing relevance.

How Interested I am

Not

Not

Where INTEREST = all $(me)^2 + I$

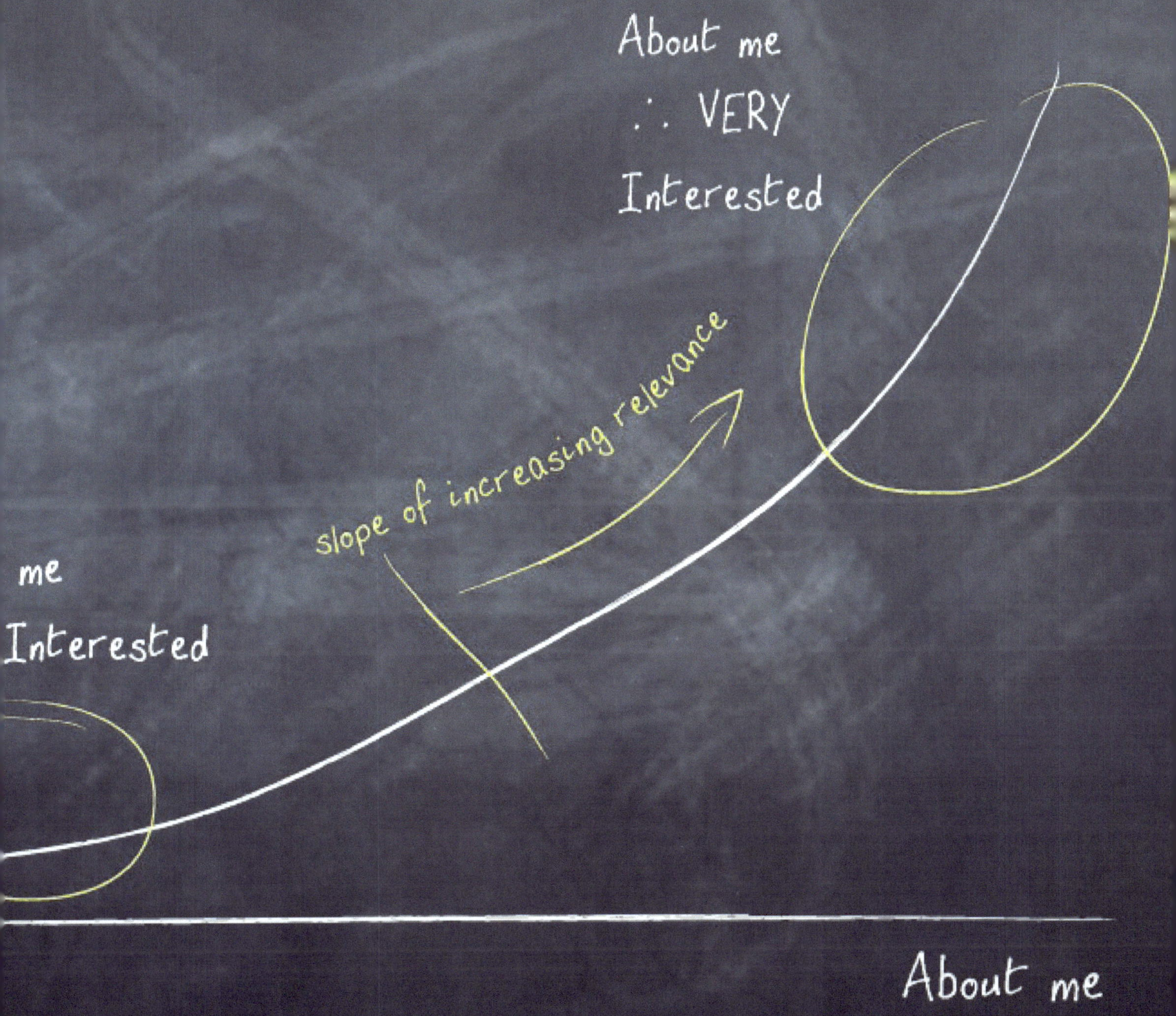

Once upon a time there were three bears who lived in a cottage in the woods. There was a Papa Bear, a medium-sized Mama Bear, and a Baby Bear.

One morning the three bears made porridge for breakfast. But it was too hot to eat, the

Rule #3
Tell a Story

Rule #3 falls into the category of easy to say, hard to do. Unless we work in a particularly creative business, storytelling doesn't seem like honest business-related work. It seems like something we should be doing at home with our kids. And we are so used to PowerPoint, we've forgotten what a story is and how to tell it.

Stories have power – the power to engage, the power to educate, the power to move. The right stories give people the power to believe and the power to act. It's been that way since the stone age; people huddled around campfires and invented language. It's how we humans relate to each other.

facts { *The King died, then the Queen died* } story
of a broken heart.

E.M.Forster
Aspects of the Novel

E.M. Forster talks about the difference between lifeless facts and a story in "Aspects of the Novel". Look at this bald statement: The King and the Queen died. Now, listen to this tiny story: The King died and then the Queen died of a broken heart. Which is more interesting? More emotional? Which will you remember? Persuade with stories.

We worked with a client who was the Chief Operating Officer of a Fortune 500 company that ran retail distribution. On one store visit, he found a messy bathroom. The bathroom was for employees, but customers used them. Jack takes up the story, "So I decided to clean the bathroom. I hung up my jacket, got the cleaning supplies out and started scrubbing. I was in there such a long time I think the store manager thought I had a heart attack. When he came into the bathroom and saw me with my sleeves rolled up, cleaning, he just about had a heart attack."

Why does Jack tell that story? It humanizes him. It says that even though he has a big important title, he rolls up his sleeves and does what it takes to get the job done. For him, it's an object lesson in focusing on the details. If you get the little things right, the big things follow. It's not about what your job is. It is about what you're responsible for. This story has transcended into myth in Jack's company and now spotless bathrooms are everywhere!

Jack could have put a bullet on a slide stressing the importance of keeping the stores clean, but he doesn't. Somehow, PowerPoint gives us permission to stop being people. Human interest gets replaced by bullets, spread sheets and clip art. Stories – and energy, engagement and stimulation – magically vanish. And we wonder why the audience is bored.

HOOK   **MEAT**   **PAYOFF**

That story has to have a structure to it. For a presentation, think of three acts. Act one is the Hook. (More on that later). Act two is the meat of the presentation, how you organize your argument. Finally, act three is the payoff; this is where you sum up your case, recap, or ask the ask. If you do it well, you'll find it's the payoff for your Hook.

Whatever you are going to say, use a story to say it. It can be a personal story that establishes your credibility. Or someone else's story that highlights a particular opportunity or problem. Stories work. Use them.

Rule #4
Every Slide has a **Point**

Rule #4 is simple; every slide has a point. Use this rule to edit the flow of your deck. If you're stuck, get a colleague to ask you, "What's the point of this slide". You should be able to answer. Write that answer down. If you don't know the point of the slide, you don't have a slide. If you can't make the point of the slide simply, in a sentence or two, you don't have a slide.

Rule #5
Set Your Hook

All great stories have a great beginning. "It was the best of times; it was the worst of times." "Call me Ishmael." You won't get to the level of Charles Dickens or Herman Melville, but you can take a page from their books. Set the hook for your presentation at the outset.

A great hook does two things; it gets your audience leaning forward, and it gives them a context for what's to come. Most business presentations don't do this. The standard start is an agenda. Let me tell you what I am going to cover today. That's a recipe for sitting back and settling in, not leaning forward.

One of the best examples of a hook comes from the movies. I was 11 years old when Star Wars came out. I can still remember the excitement as I read about "a long time ago in a galaxy far, far away". Then the opening notes of the soundtrack blasted through the theatre. I was hooked. It drew me in and set the stage with the opening crawl:

> *"It is a period of civil war. Rebel spaceships, striking from a hidden base, have won their first victory against the evil GALACTIC EMPIRE. During the battle, Rebel spies managed to steal secret plans to the Empire's ultimate weapon, the DEATH STAR, an armored space station with enough power to destroy an entire planet. Pursued by the Empire's sinister agents, Princess Leia races home aboard her starship, custodian of the stolen plans that can save her people and restore freedom to the galaxy..."*

Thirty years have gone by. But that crawl, that music, and that imagery of a massive spacecraft pursued by an even bigger one in the opening effects – that was the hook to a $30 billion franchise. You may not be George Lucas, but you can work hard on your hook. You only have one chance to make a first impression.

If there is only one part of your presentation you practice, it has to be this one. A smooth and engaging start will immediately relax you, allowing you to have a more effective presentation. And it will get your audience up and running with you. It's not easy to break through and get people engaged. But it's much harder to bring them in if you have a bumpy start...

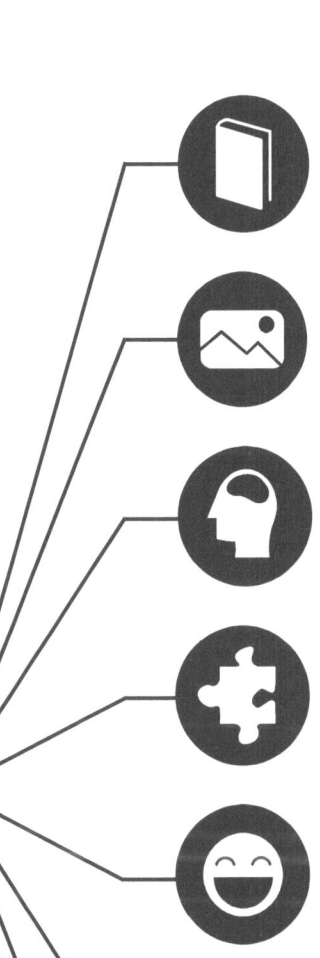

STORY
Usually a personal story that relates to the subject at hand. It humanizes the speaker and gives them credibility on a subject.

VIDEO/ GRAPHIC
Pictures can be worth a thousand words and grab your audience at the same time. They are useful to carry through the theme of your talk.

BELIEF STATEMENT
A pithy statement that captures your views on the topic and entices the audience to come on the journey.

INTRIGUING STRUCTURE
Laying out the highs and lows (and the path between) of your story upfront, can create a sense of drama.

HUMOR
Difficult to pull off, in the right hands it's a mixture of a provocation and surprise, wrapped together and delivered well.

RHETORICAL QUESTION
A way to get the audience thinking and bring them into your presentation easily. "What's your ...?"

PROVOCATIVE STATEMENT
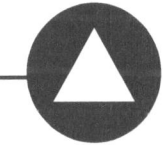
The edgier kissing cousin to the belief statement, it's a stimulating point of view that opens up the presentation.

SHOCK/ SURPRISE

Get your audience on the edge of their seats (in a good way) and hearts thumping, with a shock or surprise (particularly a fact).

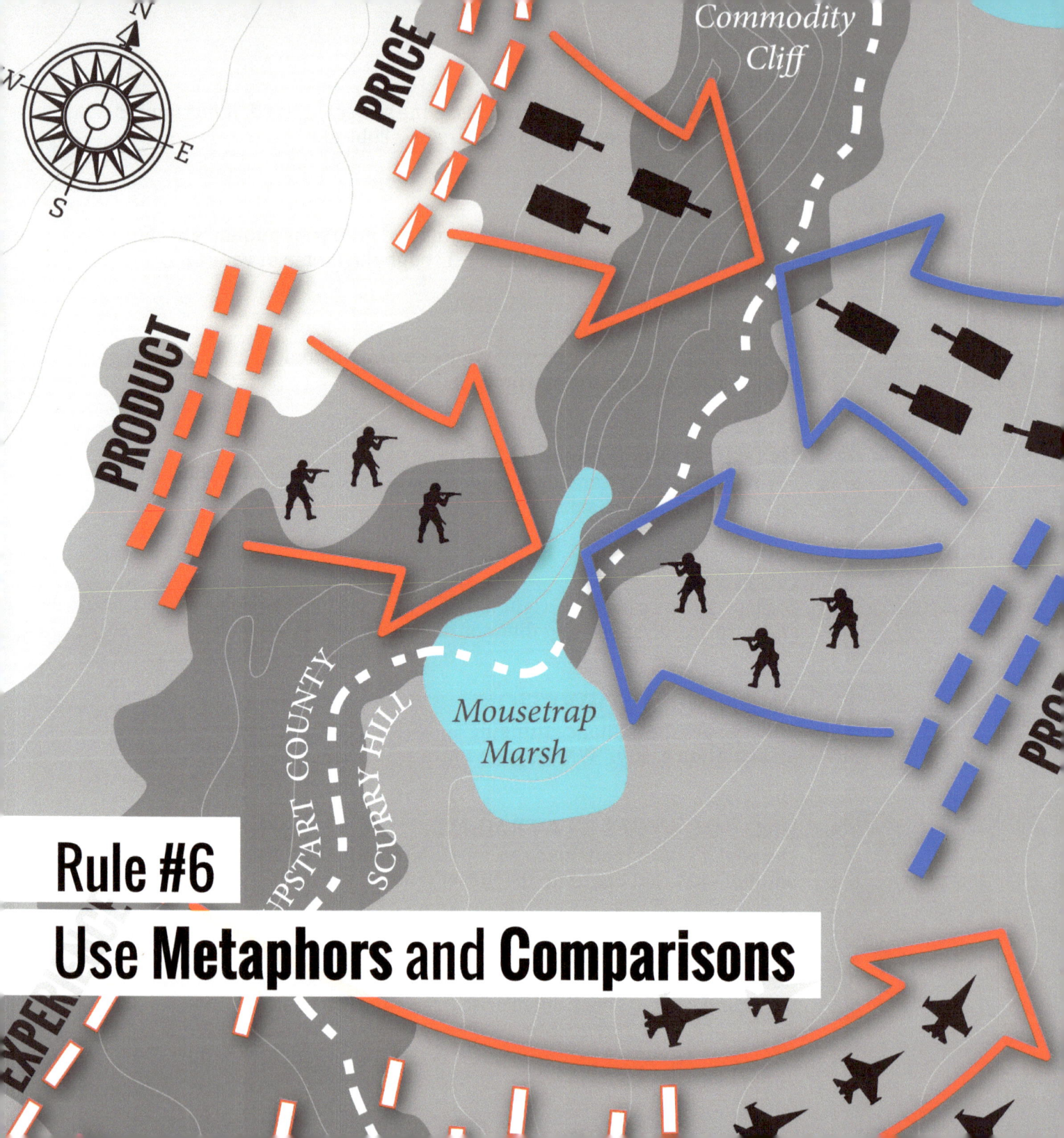

Rule #6
Use **Metaphors** and **Comparisons**

Here's a little problem you will have with your next presentation. You know too much and you're too passionate about it. On the face of it, that doesn't sound like a problem. But consider that your audience (refer to rules 1 and 2) doesn't know as much as you and isn't as interested in the subject as you are. How do you bridge that gap? That's where metaphors and comparisons come in.

If you're dealing with a complex or abstract concept, you want to make it appear real to the audience. You want to breathe life into it, and add layers of meaning. That's what analogies, metaphors and comparisons do. Think about the trifecta this way. The analogy is for a complex argument. The metaphor is a simple turn of phrase that makes the argument come alive (more vivid and less Frankenstein). The comparison is for numbers.

The purpose of the analogy is to take an abstract subject seem real. Consider these two statements:

Businesses compete with each other, with different products, price points, and service levels.

Businesses compete on three battlefields; price, product and customer experience.

There are no analogies in the first statement, but the second introduces an analogy — the battlefield — that shapes your thinking. First, the competition is suddenly a lot fiercer. Second, there is distinction between the battlefields. Throw in a juicy metaphor or two; *Competing on price is trench warfare. A game of inches where we never make any real progress. It's a race to the bottom.*

Next time you see someone make a presentation, or hear a speech, look for the use of analogy and metaphor.

Humans don't do well with big numbers and abstract concepts.

If we can't see it or touch it, it's difficult to wrap our heads around it. That's a problem for you as a presenter, when you're often challenged with dealing with big numbers. *Our growth rate for our cloud services was over 700k last quarter or small numbers, we had a .1 basis point decrease in our churn. Or abstract concepts, our data analysis shows a correlation between customer experience, AHT and repeat visits.*

Because we spend so much time preparing our presentations and are usually the expert in the room, it's easy to forget this. We throw around ARPU, 432,000, 2 basis points, and data architecture like it's confetti, ignoring the glazed looks.

You're looking for 3 elements to make a good comparison. Think of them as the *object,* the *multiple* and the *contrast.* The *object* is the big (small) number or abstract concept you're comparing. The *multiple* is the factor which makes that comparison. The *contrast* is the known object you're comparing to.

A couple of tips to make your comparison work.

Pick a contrast that's real and makes sense for the quality you're trying to compare. For instance, if you're searching to make height real, you might say, "the Burj Khalifa is the world's tallest building at 2,717 feet. That's over 100 times taller than the average house." Saying, "it's eight thousand times taller than a mouse" would sound stupid. You're highlighting tall as a quality. To you, a two story house is tall. A mouse is small.

Make the connection to the contrast emotional. It should line up to what you're going for. For instance, "Our website got 50,000 visitors yesterday. That's enough to fill Yankee Stadium." A visit to Yankee Stadium is much more visceral than "enough to fill three parking lots".

Make the multiple small. Use 1-3, or 10. Don't bother when it gets into the 100's, it get's difficult to comprehend. At a push, use 1000 or 100 times. For instance, "the threat level to our network has ramped up. We now average 7 attacks per day." That's easier to understand and remember than the shorter, we had 2,564 discrete attacks on our network last year".

Pick "real" language over precise. "We hired 5,200 new employees last year, that's more people than the Newco acquisition." Using the word people is better than employees, is better than the more accurate FTE's. Say, "That's about 3 times..." versus, " ... 3.1 times".

Never contrast a difficult grok with another. For example, explaining the U.S. Debt by using multiples of a billion is useless because we can't get our heads around a billion. You have to take it in steps. Likewise, it's difficult when you get to Exabytes and Yottabytes.

OVER LOAD OVER LOAD OVER LOAD

STOP STOP STOP

START START

Rule #7
Headlines Beat Labels

Click to add headline

If I could change one thing about PowerPoint for the better, I would remove the "click to add title" and make it "click to add headline." Maybe, just maybe, it might make people stop and think. Instead of plugging in what passes for a title on your next PowerPoint deck — *4th Quarter Highlights, Consolidated Quarterly Reviews, Traffic Earning Costs,* there might be an actual, exciting, point-making, "I get it, now I'm interested", aha, honest to goodness headline.

Most people forget that PowerPoint has the word **point** in it, and they are trying to make a point. In the news industry, a headline like, "Headless Body Found in Topless Bar" sold newspapers. In the world of blogging and SEO, a headline has to work for humans and algorithms. If it's not effective, you're not getting eyeballs. In the world of PowerPoint, it has to make the point. You're looking for self-explanatory (like a label) and catchy (to appeal to people). For instance, you could label a slide on unemployment in the US, *Unemployment in US since 2004*, or headline it *Unemployment: Are you better off?*

Most people default to a label.

Your first warning sign should be the number of words. If it isn't a sentence, or at least doesn't read like a sentence, you have a label. You can tell — it will be short, usually a couple of words, and categorize the information on the slide. Labels are good for charts, bad for slides.

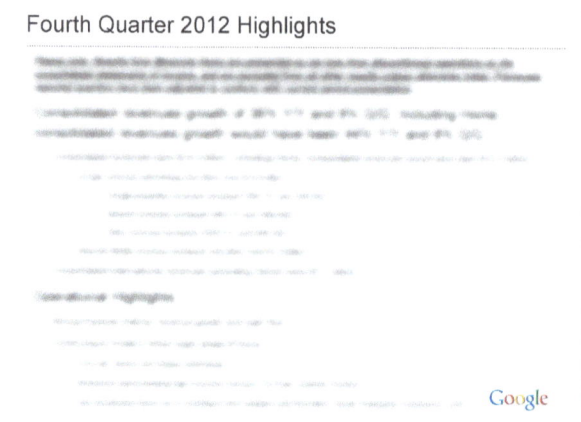

Fourth Quarter 2012 Highlights

Here's an example from a company that most look to as an example of how it's done. Not in this case. It's a slide from Google's 2012 fourth quarter earnings call. I've blurred out the content, so you can focus on the title. It's a label. A label tells you what the slide is about, but it doesn't tell you anything else. You don't know the point of the slide, apart from the subject matter ("here are the highlights from our fourth quarter"). Good to know, but it shouldn't be the title of your slide. Since everyone has highlights from their 4th quarter, it's not distinctive.

What's in a Headline?

A good headline will do the work for you. In a crisp way, it will make the point you want to make. It's both self-explanatory and catchy.

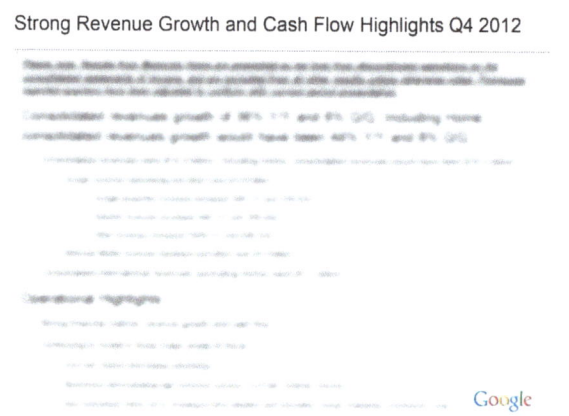

Strong Revenue Growth and Cash Flow Highlights Q4 2012

How do you go from a label to a headline. A simple question, "What do you want people to get from this slide?" will give you an answer that leads to your headline. It doesn't need to be a complete sentence, but shoot for sentence-like. Don't worry if you have to wrap a couple of lines.

Label-check.

So here's a handy tip when you're working through your deck. Take a glance at your deck and count the number of labels vs. headlines. Step 2, rework the label to a headline. If you have the nasty habit of putting a bottom line or take-away in the body of your slide, your path to reform is clear. Just turn it into a headline. If you don't, you probably have the headline buried in the body of your slide somewhere. This is handy, as a) you don't have to work too hard to find it, and b) you can take some of the clutter out of your slide.

Here's some more from the Google deck, which is all labels. In contrast, here's a company I normally wouldn't hold up as a benchmark, but for their earnings results, they've done a better job of using headlines.

3Q12 Highlights: Strong Growth in Broadband, Both Wireless and Wireline Data

Michael Alley, Professor of Engineering and presentation auteur at Penn State defined the assertion-evidence model. His research found that a compelling crisp headline in sentence form, backed up by evidence (usually visual) in the main body of a slide, increases comprehension and recall. That's the power of a good headline. It doesn't always work, and some famous headlines have been ignored — *Bin Laden Poised to Attack US* springs to mind — but a headline will at least work for you.

Rule #8
Know **Where** You Want the Eye to Go

It doesn't matter how great a presenter you are, there's a limit to what the audience can and will take in. Neuroscientists call that working memory storage capacity. While they can't agree why this limit exists, they do agree that we're limited to about three to five "chunks" of information.[1] Sadly this means that no matter how fantastic the advice here, you'll only remember three things.

It's why, when you remember a phone number, you will remember it in three "chunks" 203 - 555 - 7172, not 2035557172. We want to make this work for us in the slides we're building.

---

[1] Cowan, Nelson. "The Magical Mystery Four: How Is Working Memory Capacity Limited, and Why?" N.p., n.d. Web.
Miyake, Akira, and Priti Shah. Models of Working Memory: Mechanisms of Active Maintenance and Executive Control. Cambridge: Cambridge UP, 1999. Web.
Mayer, Richard E. The Cambridge Handbook of Multimedia Learning. Cambridge, U.K.: Cambridge UP, 2005. Print.

You know the main point of the slide, but there's still a lot of other information to convey. Your job is to chunk it out into an information hierarchy. Think about it in tiers —

Level 1, the Headline, is more important than

Level 2, the sub points and supporting bullets than

Level 3, the supporting details.

What you want is someone to "get" what your slide is about at a glance. Spending a few minutes listening to the speaker, or reading the slide will give the audience more information. Finally, they will get detail.

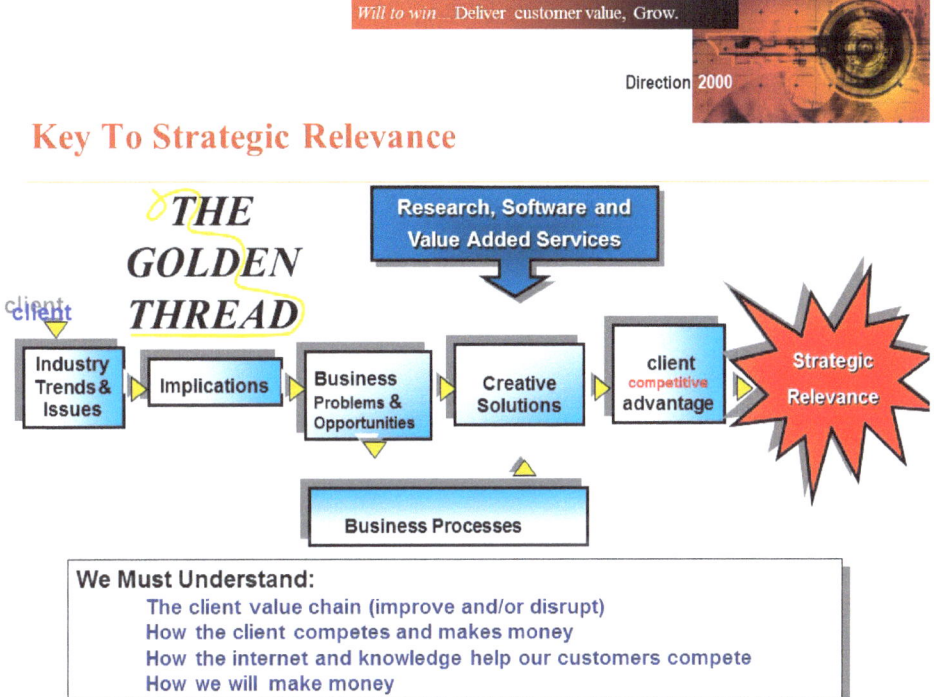

This is a bad example. I didn't create that slide and, without someone leading me through it, I have no idea what the main point is. Is it strategic relevance? The golden thread? The process? It just isn't clear to me.

Rule #9
The **Eight Foot** Rule

Excessive squinting, headaches, general irritableness? Your audience may be suffering from PowerPoint Myopia. It's a condition we're all victims of. It happens when we try to put too much on the slide, and meekly apologize, "this may be difficult to see in the back." In crowded rooms, you'll also see bottom blindness, where your audience can't see the bottom part of the slide because it's obscured by someone's head. After years of research, we may have found a cure to this appalling malady.

When creating slides and decks, I don't have a rule for text size or how big stuff should be. Instead, around our office, we have the 8ft. Rule.

The **8** ft rule

Because you don't give presentations like this...

Rule #10

Use **Structure, Words** and **Pictures**

STRUCTURE

WORDS

PICTURES

If you have a favorite TV show or movie, you have seen masters of communication at work. A whole crew of people — the actors, directors, producers, cinematographers and scriptwriters — who collaborate together to bring you into their world. You've also seen a presentation or two where you got lost, confused or just bored. That's the other end of the scale.

What's happening in your favorite movie, and not happening in that bad presentation is the artful blending of *Structure, Words* and *Pictures*.

In the movie business, that goes under a different name. The *Words* are the screenplay or dialogue. The *Structure* is the plot, the acts or scenes, the *Pictures* are the cinematography, the special effects and art direction. You know it when you see it, the dance of *Words, Pictures* and *Structure* that brings you a great show.

When one of those elements is missing, or weak, you have a bad movie. It's like watching a bad Hong Kong action movie — no plot, bad dialogue, wooden acting and the character's lines out of sync with their mouths.

This tragedy happens in presentations. The *Words* and *Pictures* may be amazing, but you can't follow the logical structure of what the presenter is asking you to learn or do. Or the *Structure* may make sense, and you understand the *Words*, but it's so dull and dry you have trouble staying awake.

What you have to work on is the *Structure* of your presentation — the Hook, Meat and Payoff. Then make sure every slide has a point, and you say it in an emotional way. Use real words, not corporate pig-latin. Remember we are fundamentally visual creatures. Our ability to retain and understand increases massively if we put pictures in with the words and create an experience.

Anyone who has carried a bag of samples around and made customer sales visits will tell you that monologues don't make money. Dialogues do. A conversation. If you show up in a customer's doorway and you're the one doing all the talking, you've talked yourself out of the sale. Same with your presentation. Find ways to get your audience engaged. Ask real questions. Pay attention to their needs. Don't just rely on slides. Go to a flipchart, play a film clip or bring another voice into the room. Change the pace.

Follow these 10 simple rules to change your PowerPoint Karma and have a leadership conversation.